AF224250

Lizzy 'N Dizzy

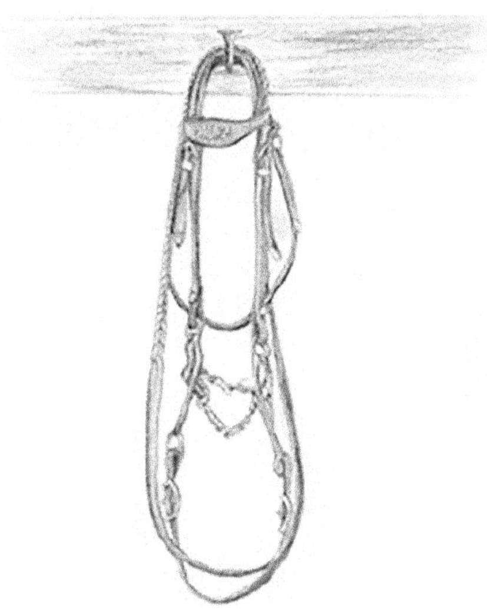

Joyce Lambert

Illustrated by Jan Metzger-Hartwig

Special Thanks To:
Susan, who keeps me on track with editing, design and content.
Carol, who is my proofreader, and tech support.
Jan, whose illustrative talent still amazes me!

In memory of my mother
My biggest supporter
Beverly June Graves
June 2, 1919 - July 9, 2017

Contents

1

Love of Horses

ELIZABETH EPONA PENDERGASS PULLED at the tie of her school uniform. She felt as if it were choking the life out of her, just like this stuffy private school. How she had endured another year she would never know. She just had to get through this last week, and then she would be out of the congestion of the city and in the country with her grandparents. As soon as the school bell rang, Elizabeth shot out of her seat and dashed for the door.

"Miss Pendergass, <u>decorum</u> if you please!" A severe-looking teacher scolded Elizabeth for her hasty departure. Slowing down she kept her focus on her objective, the door. Today was Wednesday, and that meant going to the stables for her riding lessons.

Jake, Elizabeth's chauffeur, was waiting with the car. He was ever-faithful arriving with the long black Lincoln Continental stretch limousine. Her parents never picked her up. Elizabeth wasn't even sure they could find their way to the school, but she didn't let it bother her anymore. Not like it did when she was little. She would watch other parents welcome their children with open arms and big smiles, but not hers. They were the Pendergasses, after all. They did not believe in any public show of emotions, let alone affection. Oh, Elizabeth knew her parents loved her, even if she was a girl. (They had a hard time hiding the disappointment of her gender; who would carry on the family name?) They just had a different way of showing love, like by giving her riding lessons. Even if the lessons were riding with decorum in an English saddle, it meant she could be with her beloved horse.

Elizabeth loved horses much more than she loved people. Since her first wish for a pony at the age of six, she had been consumed with her love of horses. Her first riding lesson was on a fat dapple-gray pony named Prince. (It was hard to believe that was six years ago.) Now, the horse she rode was a very tall <u>thoroughbred</u>. Her mount at the present was Mr. Majestic Thunder. How he got that name Elizabeth could not understand, as there was nothing thunderous about him, unless one counted the blaze on his face that looked like a bolt of lightning. He was always happy to see her and greeted her with a loud whinny, which would invariably get rewarded with horse candy that tasted like apples.

Jessica, her personal maid, was waiting at the barn for Elizabeth to help her change into her riding clothes. Jessica pulled Elizabeth's hair back into such a tight bun that she swore she would end up with slanted eyes.

Elizabeth's riding coach was a multi-gold-medal winner, named Stefan Narcis, a very no-nonsense kind of guy. Nothing he could say or do could damper her joy of riding. "Miss Pendergass, sit up straight, arms up, elbows in!" So it went, girl and horse, around and around the course, as she listened, was corrected, and sat stiff and proper — just like the rest of her life.

2

Freedom

ON THE LAST DAY of school, Elizabeth found it extremely difficult to pay attention. Ever since the first bell had rung, she was excited for the day to end. Today was the day she was leaving to spend the summer with her grandparents while her mother and father toured Europe, again. They had intended to take her with them as they had in the past; and on these occasions, Elizabeth and Jessica spent most of their time at the parks, at museums, or in the hotel suite playing board games or reading while her parents went to parties, teas, late-night operas, and theater. It wasn't the type of vacation she relished. (No thank you!) She did quite a bit of <u>cajoling</u> to talk her parents into letting her stay with her grandparents. Her heart sang when they finally said, "Yes."

Grandmother and Grandfather Pendergass were from one of the oldest families of Boston. They could trace their family tree back to England, where they were distantly related to royalty.

The final bell of the school year rang, and Elizabeth was out of her chair in a flash. She careened around the doorpost and ran right into the head mistress.

"Miss Pendergass, would you like to spend the next hour in the <u>demerit</u> room?"

"No, madam," Elizabeth answered with eyes downcast.

"You are excused," the head mistress uttered.

"Thank you," Elizabeth replied, as she picked up where she left off, in her hurry to escape the school.

Jake was there, as always, this time leaning on a Lincoln Navigator SUV. Jessica was with him, and the car was packed to the roof. They both smiled when they saw her, which gave Elizabeth a warm secure feeling. Jessica asked how school was and wanted to see her final report. "They mail that later," Elizabeth answered as she stripped off her tie and blazer. She resisted the urge to throw them up into the air or better yet, into the garbage. A quick change in the car made the trip much more comfortable.

"Ready?" Jake said with a twinkle in his eye.

"Way past ready. Thunder is already there! Father had him shipped yesterday, and I can't wait to see him," Elizabeth enthusiastically replied.

"Well, buckle up and let's go!" Jake encouraged, as everyone climbed into the SUV. Elizabeth pushed the button opening the moon roof, letting the warm spring sunshine bathe the interior of the vehicle.

Watching the landscape change from tall imposing buildings to tall majestic trees of every variety made Elizabeth fall asleep. She woke to a gentle nudging and a soft whisper calling, "Lizzy, Lizzy, are you hungry?"

An automatic smile came to Elizabeth's face. She loved to be called Lizzy. The only one to ever do it was Jessica, when no one was around. It just wasn't done; it wasn't proper, especially coming from a maid. Elizabeth rubbed the sleep from her eyes and sat up slowly. For a moment, the view left her speechless. "Where are we?"

"We are just crossing the Kentucky state line," was Jake's answer for the query.

"It is amazing! I love it!" Elizabeth could hardly contain her excitement.

"How long before we get there?" she wondered out loud.

"About two more hours," Jake answered with a laugh.

"Two hours? This trip is taking forever! I can't wait much longer!" she remarked rolling down her window and sticking out her head.

"Okay, Elizabeth," Jake chided, "Get your head back in the car, please." Elizabeth would do anything for Jake and Jessica. Sometimes she wished they were her parents.

After a quick bite to eat, the travelers were back on the road. Elizabeth did not fall asleep this time. She watched out the window for anything she could remember.

She had only been to her grandparents' farm once, but she was too little to remember. Her mother and father were not impressed with the rolling hills and the smells of the country. They preferred the orderly existence of the city. No singing birds (who could not tell time), or crowing roosters (who were simply obnoxious), or any other sounds that did not resemble traffic, horns, whistles or trains; but that is what Elizabeth remembered the most about the country-side, the sounds and the smells. It was not like the old smell of hay in the stable where she took her lessons. It was fresh cut hay, grass and flowers. She had never smelled anything like it, except poor imitation air fresheners.

Finally, the big wrought-iron gates came into view, proclaiming, "**_Epona_ Estates.**" Elizabeth always wondered if the farm was named after her or the other way around.

Jake pulled up and pressed the intercom button. "Yes?" was the bodiless query.

"Miss Pendergass to see the elders," Jake responded in his formal voice.

"Please enter at a sedate speed," were the emotionless instructions. As the huge gates swung open, Jake put the SUV in gear and slowly drove to the main house. Elizabeth's mouth fell open. *They call this a little farm in the country?* The sign on the way in was much more accurate, "Estate." The house was complete with tennis courts, a swimming pool, a lap pool, a sixteen bay garage, and stables that seemed miles long. Elizabeth got out of the SUV slowly. She could hardly take it all in at one time. She didn't even notice a pair of excited elderly people coming toward her.

"Elizabeth!" her grandmother called with open arms. That caught Elizabeth's attention, and she hurried to the warm welcome.

"I thought I would never get here. I'm glad we had a short school day."

"Well, you are here now!" her grandmother said with a smile. "Jake, you and Jessica come on up to the house, and I'll send someone for the bags. Come on Dearie; let's get you settled. Why don't you run on up to the second floor and pick out the bedroom you would like to call your own?" Grandmother Elaine winked over Elizabeth's head at Jessica. Elizabeth did not need any more prompting; she raced into the house and up the open arm staircase.

3

Feels Like Home

ELIZABETH BEGAN OPENING DOORS, ignoring the double doors at the end, because something told her that was her grandparent's room. The first door on the right was decorated in pink roses. The second was lavender wisteria or lilacs or something like that. The third was paneled in dark wood and had a large canopied bed. Next was the Chinese room. It had jade and red curtains, black furniture, and even a small Confucius on the dresser. Then Elizabeth opened the door to the chintz room. This room was bright and sunny with lemony stripes and yellow buttercup flowers on most of the materials in the room. Finally, she opened the fifth door, and knew she need not to look any further. The walls were soft beige with sage borders around the windows, doors and top of the walls. A chair rail was around the room and above it was a border of horses.

I bet Grandmother had a hand in this; Elizabeth thought to herself.

Every breed of horse that could ever be named or mentioned was pictured. Each breed showed a different pose of stallion, mare, and foal. Better yet, they were discretely labeled. Jessica and Grandmother Pendergass found Elizabeth engrossed in reading all the names of the horses that frolicked around the room. "Elizabeth," they called in unison, but got no response. Again, they said her name, but were not answered. "Lizzy!" Jessica called. With that, everyone stopped and looked at Jessica with full attention and surprise. Jessica turned toward Mrs. Pendergass in shock, realizing what she had called Elizabeth, "I beg your pardon," she pleaded.

"Lizzy. I like the sound of that. It fits her to a tee," said Grandmother. She turned and looked into her granddaughter's eyes and smiled. "I'll have the bags brought up for you… Lizzy."

Elizabeth said with a great sigh, "Thank you, Grandmother, and I love my room!" She turned to take in more of its details, "How did you know I was coming? I just found out for sure yesterday!"

"Oh, Honey, we have had this room ready for you for years. We just change it according to the age you are each year. We knew someday your parents would let you come. I couldn't be happier to finally have you here."

"Don't ever change the room again; I love it just the way it is right now!"

"You may change your mind as you grow older," Grandmother chided.

"No! I won't! It's perfect!" Elizabeth reassured her grandmother.

"Very well, Dear, I won't change a thing until you ask," Mrs. Pendergass assured her granddaughter. With that, Elizabeth hugged her grandmother with all the pent-up love she felt for years, while a single tear fell from her grandmother's smiling eyes.

Someone brought up the baggage, and Jessica put everything away. It felt like coming home, which was odd since Elizabeth had been here only once before. Everyone began calling Elizabeth "Lizzy," and she basked in its sounding so normal. This summer was going to be even greater than she had hoped. *Lizzy.* Yes, Elizabeth really liked that name.

4

Summer For Riding

LIZZY'S GOLD-MEDAL WINNING COACH showed up the third day of her vacation. He was appalled when Lizzy showed up at the stable in her new jeans, a recent gift from her grandmother. "Young lady, you will go put on proper riding attire immediately, or there will be no lesson!" Stefan insisted.

Just as Lizzy was about to argue, Jessica simply said, "Come, Miss," and that was that. As they were getting out her riding clothes, Jessica explained, "Lizzy, Stefan has your parent's ear. If he tells them you are not acting like a young lady, your days here will be numbered. So do what he tells you without backtalk, please."

"Okay, Jessie," Lizzy said.

"And don't let him hear you call me Jessie!" her maid reminded her.

Lizzy took what Jessica said to heart. She did *not* want to jeopardize her wonderful summer. So, she was the picture of decorum whenever her riding coach Stefan was around, right down to her knee-high, spit polished riding boots.

5

Bad News

LIZZY SIMPLY GLOWED. THIS summer was starting out better than she had ever imagined. There were some things she could do without, like the formal dinner every night, which was something her grandmother had insisted. "It keeps us from reverting to the uncivilized, plus it makes the transition back to Boston that much easier," Grandmother explained. So every evening they all got dressed up in their Sunday best for dinner. The table was set in the proper fashion, with three forks, two knives, and three spoons. With that came three plates, and two bowls along with two glasses and a cup, topped off with a dessert fork and plate. All was exquisite china, silver, and crystal, but even this dinner arrangement couldn't dampen Lizzy's wonderful summer.

Lizzy couldn't contain her enthusiasm when she caught her first fish. It happened when Grandfather Augustus (Gus)Pendergass asked Lizzy if she liked to fish. When she told him she had never been fishing, he told her they had better remedy that, and it was just what they did. Although Lizzy did not bait her own hook, she did catch a great big bass. It was as if catching that fish opened a flood gate of communication between Lizzy and her grandfather, because since that moment, she could not stop talking a mile a minute. Grandfather didn't have the heart to tell her the talking probably meant the end to catching any more fish. He just sat back in his seat and thoroughly enjoyed her chatter. He discovered how lonely she had been most her life. Grandfather resolved that he, and Grandmother would take a more active role in Lizzy's life from now on, even after she returned to Boston. They would still attend school functions, and her riding events like they had been, but in between; they would spend more time with her. That decided, Grandfather could really relax and enjoy the rest of the day.

Grandmother Elaine acted very pleased when the day's catch was presented to the cook, but when Gus told Elaine the biggest fish was Lizzy's, the <u>accolades</u> really began. "Are you kidding me? On your first time, you out-fished your grandfather? I'm sure he will insist on another chance to redeem himself," Grandmother said with a laugh.

The cook fixed the fish to perfection. Lizzy could not believe she had helped catch what they were eating. She didn't think things could get much better. Then the phone rang. It was for Stefan with news that would change the rest of her summer.

The news that was delivered the next morning left everyone in a daze. A horse had kicked one of the Olympic riders, and it broke his arm in two places. Because Stefan was an alternate for the <u>equestrian</u> team, the Olympic Committee called him to fill the void. He said he was sorry to say that there would be no more lessons for Elizabeth this summer.

Lizzy didn't know how to respond to the news. If the truth were known, she didn't like Stefan all that much, but he knew riding. Now Lizzy didn't know who would teach or help her with Thunder. Grandfather patted Lizzy's hand and said, "Don't worry honey, these things have a way of working themselves out. Let's wait to see what tomorrow brings."

Lizzy found it very hard to sleep that night. She kept thinking of what her summer would be like with no riding. She tossed and turned and drank six glasses of water, which only made her have to use the bathroom three times. All in all, it was a very long sleepless night.

6

Shoeing Day

AT THE BREAKFAST TABLE, Grandmother took one look at Lizzy and said, "You look awful. Did you get any sleep at all?"

"No, I don't think so, and if I did, I don't feel it. Did Grandfather come up with a solution?" was her tired reply.

"I don't think he was worried. He said it will work itself out, and I think it will too," Grandmother tried to reassure her.

"May I be excused?" Lizzy asked. "I would like to see Thunder and explain why I won't be riding today."

"Yes, Dear, and take some horse candy to make him feel better," Grandmother encouraged. Lizzy's trip to the stable seemed to take twice as long. There was no pep in her step, or pride in her stride; she just ambled on, slowly and steadily.

When she arrived at the barn, there was a flurry of activity. People were laughing and talking, and horses were stomping. It made Lizzy wonder what was going on; didn't they know the terrible thing that had happened? She followed the sounds until she came to the hitching rail at the far end of the barn. There, parked just outside the door, was a truck she had never seen before. "What's going on?" she asked when she saw her grandfather.

"Oh, nothing unusual. Ed Thomas is just here for shoeing day," he answered.

"What is shoeing day?" Lizzy inquired.

"Well, every six or eight weeks, the <u>farrier</u> comes to replace the shoes on some of the horses. We have too many to do in one day, so he will come Monday and Wednesday this week to get them all done," Grandfather explained.

"Thunder wears shoes, but I was never there when they were put on. May I watch?" she asked.

"Of course, if you're not too busy. It takes a little while," he said.

"I have all day since I won't be taking a lesson," she sadly responded.

Grandfather wasn't sure what tired out Ed more, shoeing the horses or answering all of Lizzy's questions. Before the first half-hour was over, Lizzy forgot she was sad and depressed. She found the whole business of shoeing fascinating. "Why are those shoes so flat?" was one of the questions she asked.

"These are called slide plates; they are used for reining horses, so they can turn on a dime and do a sliding stop," Ed patiently answered.

"Why would they want to do that?" was Lizzy's next query.

"Well, sometimes it is just for show, but other times when the farm hands are working cattle, those maneuvers come in very handy," Ed tried to explain.

"What are these ridges on these shoes used for and why are they so much lighter than the others?" Lizzy quickly questioned the farrier.

"The ridged ones are used for traction, then a horse can dig down and really push for speed. They are light, so they don't weigh his feet down," came the reply.

"Who needs to do that?" Lizzy quizzed.

"Well, the Pony Express riders do," Ed joked.

"Even I know there are no Pony Express riders anymore," Lizzy commented back with a smile.

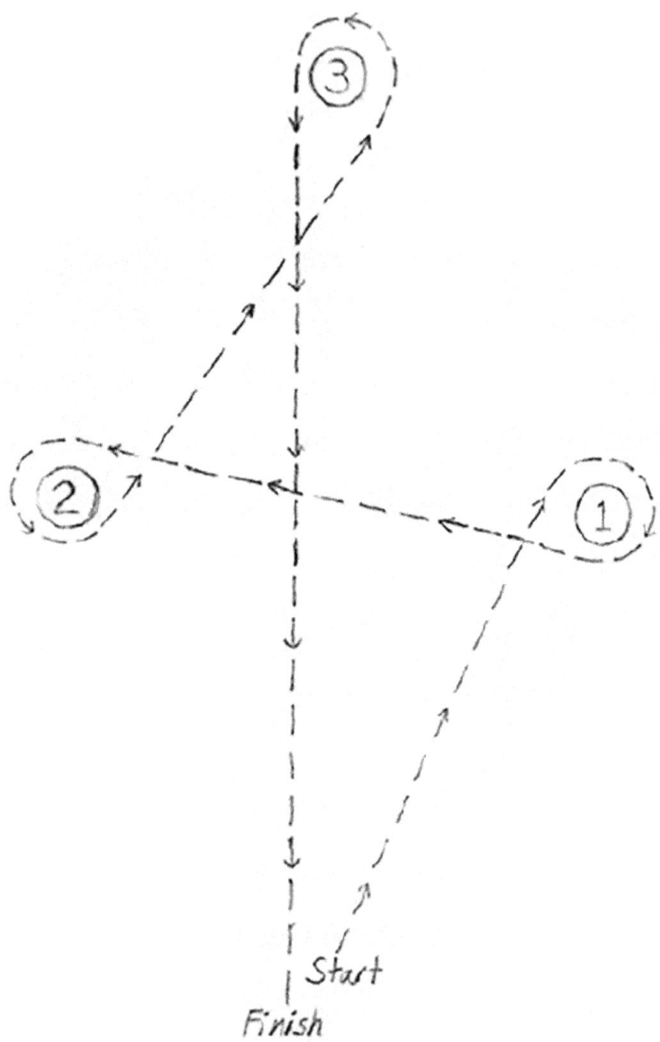

"You got me there," Ed laughed. "These are for barrel racers."

"Why would anyone want to race a barrel, and why would they need shoes like that to do it? I can't imagine a barrel going as fast as a horse unless it was rolled down a hill or something," Lizzy gave as a no-nonsense answer. The uproar of laughter made Lizzy feel a little uncomfortable. It had made perfect sense to her.

"Honey," Grandfather gently said when he sensed her discomfort, "they don't actually race the barrel. The horse and rider race around three barrels in a cloverleaf pattern for the best time." When Lizzy didn't look convinced, Grandfather said, "Come with me."

Grandfather took Lizzy to the back paddock where she could see the barrels. "Now watch as Jed takes a turn around the barrels," he instructed. Lizzy climbed atop the white rail fence to get a better look. Before she knew what to expect, the horse and rider were around the first barrel and headed to the second. It seemed as if the horse had a magnet in his nose, the turn around the barrel was so tight. The third barrel was taken in the same manner. Dirt was flying as the horse dug in to lengthen its stride in the straightaway, and Jed was encouraging his horse to go faster. The excitement was very contagious. Lizzy found herself yelling, "Go!"

Ah, Grandfather thought to himself, as Lizzy's mile-a-minute talk returned; she *isn't sad anymore.*

7

Barrel Racing

THE NEXT FEW DAYS were filled with questions about barrel racing. Who started it? How do judges tell who wins? Where do the races take place? On and on the questions came. Grandfather answered them the best he could; but when he ran out of answers, he passed the questions off to Jed. Jed was one of the best hands of the Pendergass' ranch. He loved working at Epona Estates because they allowed him to continue his barrel racing. Jed did it mostly for the love of the sport now, since he held every major award in this field. He was very happy to find someone as interested in barrel racing as he was. Jed was a quiet man and not used to being asked so many questions, but he took it all in stride and answered Lizzy in the best way she could understand.

"What are those rubber things for? Why does he have bandages on? Did your horse get hurt?" The questions continued.

"One question at a time. These aren't bandages; they are <u>splint boots</u>. They are designed to help protect the horse's legs from injury. These rubber things as you called them are <u>bell boots</u>. They are designed to keep the horse from <u>forging</u> with his shoes," Jed patiently replied. Lizzy watched as Jed saddled his horse, which brought about a whole battery of new questions.

"Why are there so many extra pieces to your saddle?" she inquired.

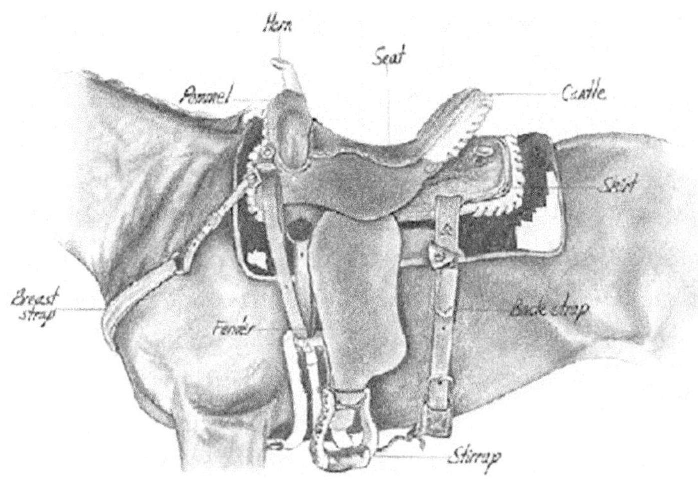

Jed rolled his eyes good-naturedly and addressed her questions. "Most saddles are alike; they have seats, skirts, pommel, cantle, stirrup straps and stirrups. This saddle also has fenders and horn, breast collar and back strap."

"Why so many more parts than my English saddle?" she asked, wanting a clearer explanation.

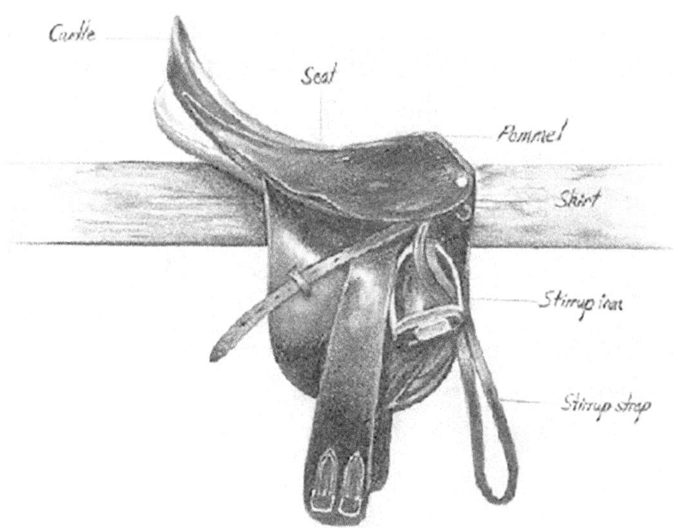

"Each part serves its own purpose. The cantle is higher to keep you from sliding off the back of the saddle. The higher pommel keeps you from sliding off the front. The horn is used for hanging on when going up steep inclines, declines or making fast turns. The fenders are to protect both the horse and the rider. The back strap and breast collar are to keep the saddle from sliding forward or backward. This is called a gaming rein. It is only one rein hooked on either side of the bit. I don't like all the extra length of regular reins when I am racing." Jed hoped these answers would satisfy her inquiring mind. It must have worked because there was a lull in the question and answer time.

Jed mounted his horse and got into the starting position. He entered the gate and circled his horse, then was off in a flash of rider, horse, and leather. Again, Jed took the turns tightly and let the horse <u>have his head</u> in the straightaway. It was even more exciting than before. Lizzy could have sat on top of that fence all day and watched different riders race around the barrels, but Grandmother was calling her on the intercom for lunch.

Grandfather had heard the summons also and pulled up to the fence in a golf cart to give Lizzy a lift to the house.

Lizzy talked all through lunch about the things Jed had told her about saddles, bridles, and all the extras. Her grandparents were happy something had taken her mind off her disappointment about her riding lessons.

It was the elder Pendergass' habit to take an hour or two rest after lunch. This gave Lizzy some time for herself. Usually Lizzy used this time to read. Sometimes she checked her laptop for emails, but most of them were forwards, and not any new or exciting news from anyone. She seemed restless and unable to settle herself down to do anything constructive. She picked up a piece of Epona Estates stationary and began a handwritten letter to her parents, something her grandmother had encouraged her to do. She told them about the ranch, the farrier, and about her riding coach being called as an alternate for the Olympic Equestrian Team. She was so animated about everything that she filled three pages before she knew it.

Jessica came in and was pleased to see Lizzy corresponding with her parents. She didn't ask what Lizzy was writing about because Jessica assumed that Lizzy missed her parents. Therefore, she agreed to mail the letter.

8

A Painful Lesson

LIZZY AND HER GRANDPARENTS went out on the boat to take her mind off her non-existent riding lessons. They had a great morning and a lunch of scrumptious fish when they got home. It was the down-times after lunch that Lizzy was having a hard time filling. She was restless and anxious all at the same time. She thought a visit to Thunder might relieve some of her energy. She put on her jeans and boots that her grandmother had bought her and headed for the barn.

After lunch everything was an eerie kind of quiet. Everyone was off doing what they were supposed to do and probably wouldn't be back until feeding time. Lizzy got the horse candy out of her pocket and rewarded Thunder for his warm whinny of welcome. Since she was alone, she began to talk to Thunder as she often did back at home. He was, after all, a very good listener. "You should see them Thunder. They practically fly around those barrels," was her excited explanation about barrel racing. "I bet you would love to do something like that." Thunder whinnied as if on cue, and one could almost see the wheels turning in Lizzy's head. "Would you like me to show you first hand?" Before the question was out of her mouth, she had already gotten down Thunder's bridle and saddle pad. Lizzy had never saddled Thunder by herself, but she had watched the groomsman do it every day. She found a <u>muck bucket</u> to stand on so she could fling the saddle over the very tall horse's back. She nearly fell off the bucket when Thunder sidestepped, but then he settled, and she regained her balance. Everything looked just as it should, if she did say so herself.

She led Thunder down the barn's main alleyway to the corral where the barrels were used. Thunder seemed a bit confused when Lizzy didn't take him to their regular riding arena, but he followed the girl he trusted and loved.

Lizzy closed the corral gate and threw the latch into place. She hadn't stopped talking the whole time she had saddled Thunder or walked him to their destination. "See, this is what I was telling you about. You start here; go around the first barrel then around the next and on to the third. Then you pick up speed to the end. Would you like to try?" Lizzy took Thunder's playing with his bit as an affirmative answer. She climbed up on the bottom rail of the fence to mount. She walked him to the spot where Jed had started his run, turned Thunder and yelled, "Yaw!" She wasn't sure what that meant, but she liked the sound of it when Jed had said it to his horse. Thunder bolted toward the first barrel, except not the way Lizzy wanted him to. He would hardly turn around the barrel at all, and when he did, it was a huge circle and the next two were no better. She felt as though things were a bit off-kilter when she kicked him into the straightaway, only to find herself very nearly underneath Thunder as his saddle slid, dumping her (very indecorously) onto the ground, Lizzy screaming as she fell. Thunder barely got stopped before he went through the fence. Her screams brought all the missing workers to her side. Jed was kneeling down next to Lizzy, while another hand had a hold of Thunder's reins trying to calm him down.

"What did you think you were doing, you little nut? Your grandfather will have my hide if you're hurt in any way," Jed spoke roughly out of concern. Lizzy's eyes were filling with tears. No one in her whole life had spoken to her like that. She wasn't sure what hurt worse, falling off the horse, or Jed's scolding.

"Oh no, you don't," Jed chided, "Don't you look at me with those big <u>Liz Taylor</u> eyes. What you did was wrong. You could have got yourself killed, let alone hurt Thunder," he said in his defense.

Lizzy was so embarrassed all she could think to say was, "Who is Liz Taylor?"

Lizzy was taken up to the house and the doctor was called, even though Lizzy told them she was all right.

"We will just check things out so your grandfather and I can have some reassurance. You don't mind, do you, Dear?" Grandmother implored. Lizzy could not refuse her grandmother, especially when she saw real concern in her eyes.

"No, if that is what you think is best," Lizzy conceded. If there were one word to describe Elizabeth, it would be *obedient*. She may disagree with some of the things her parents laid down as rules, but she respected her parents and would never defy them or her grandparents.

Jessica brought a cold compress for Lizzy's head. She wasn't going to leave Lizzy's side, even when the doctor arrived. No one knew Lizzy better than Jessica. Other than her day off, Jessica was with Lizzy 24/7. So if the doctor had any questions, Jessica would be the one to answer them. As it was, everything checked out, and Lizzy was given a clean bill of health.

Thunder, however didn't fare so well. His front heal required several stitches where he had <u>forged</u> himself. Luckily, the tendon wasn't damaged, and the veterinarian assured Jed that Thunder would make a full recovery in a short time. If Lizzy didn't feel any pain before, she did when she learned she had caused her trusted friend, Thunder, to be hurt.

9

Learning Patience

GRANDFATHER WAITED SEVERAL DAYS to let things calm down, but he knew he had to address this problem of Lizzy's impulsive actions. After all, her horse got hurt, and she could have been killed. He shuddered when that thought went through his mind. He had a plan, and he had talked about it to his wife and Jed previously. Now he had to talk to Lizzy. Grandfather knocked softly on her bedroom door. It was quiet time right after lunch, so he was sure she would be in her room.

"Come in," came the soft reply. "Hi, Grandfather. Is everything okay?"

"Well, that depends on what you define as okay," he answered. "You see, Lizzy; you gave us quite a scare the other day, and frankly, your grandmother and I don't ever want to feel that way again. You are much too precious for us to lose over something so foolhardy."

"I am sorry," Lizzy said trying to hold back the tears, "Jed made it look so easy. I guess I never considered it was dangerous." Her sincere remorse was evident.

"Well, make no mistake it was! I talked to Jed, and asked if he would teach you how to run the barrels." Lizzy came off her bed so fast her grandfather barely had time to react.

"Oh! Grandfather, you're wonderful!" Lizzy gleefully responded as she showered her grandfather with so many kisses, he thought his heart would burst!

"Jed was also right about your 'Liz Taylor' eyes," Grandfather said with a chuckle.

"Who is Liz Taylor? I asked Jed, but he was checking me for broken bones and didn't answer," Lizzy said.

"Liz Taylor is an actress with your violet-colored eyes. She made a horse movie when she was about your age called *National Velvet*," Grandfather explained. "She was horse crazy just like you."

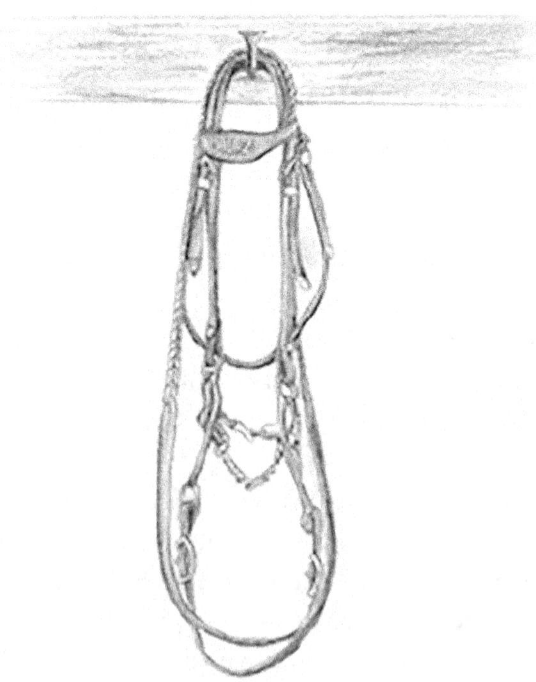

"I would love to see that movie," Lizzy remarked.

"I'll ask your grandmother to see if the local store or library has a copy. I think we would all enjoy seeing that old classic," Grandfather agreed. Sure enough, the library had a copy of the movie. So after the evening chores, they all settled down with fresh buttered popcorn to enjoy the film.

The next afternoon the lessons began. Jed instructed her on the tack differences they had discussed previously. He never treated any question as if it were foolish. After Jed laid the groundwork, and he felt comfortable with Lizzy's answers and general knowledge, he began the lessons on horseback.

Lizzy was surprised to learn she wouldn't be riding Thunder, but one of Jed's horses.

"This is Diz, one of my best friends." Jed's voice held endearing pride as he explained. "He's been with me a very long time, but I trust you to take great care with him."

"Is he gentle? Or is there a reason you call him Diz?" she asked hesitantly. "His real name is Dexter's Impressive Zip, but it's too long to say, and Zip or Zippy didn't seem to fit him. So I used his initials, D.I.Z., which he seemed to like."

"This isn't the horse you rode the other day."

"No, Diz is gettin' on in years, and I don't ride him too hard anymore."

Jed had Lizzy take a little time to talk and groom Diz, so they could get to know each other. It was plain to Jed Lizzy had not done much grooming, but she took instruction well and was a hard worker. Soon Jed could see Diz relax under Lizzy's careful attention.

Jed's "Ready?" brought Lizzy back to the present. Diz's coat had a glossy shine from the rhythmical brushing and smoothing of Lizzy's hands.

"Let's get mounted, Lizzy," Jed encouraged. Diz was not quite as tall as Thunder, and he was a bit thicker. As she sat atop his sturdy back, she noticed these differences. Jed had Lizzy walk the pattern first.

"Enter the gate. Now go to the first barrel on the right. Circle from the inside, staying close to the barrel. Now, go across the arena to the next barrel.

Circle from the topside to the left and don't let Diz have his head. Keep it close and tight, his nose toward the center of the barrel. Now come around and head to the far end of the arena to the last barrel, approaching from the right side, then bring him straight down the center to the gate to finish the cloverleaf course. Make sure you turn him at the gate or Diz will try to go all the way through it!"

Lizzy executed the instructions just as Jed had told her, and she was ready to run.

"Hold on there, young lady. There will be no running today!"

"But I did it right!" Lizzy declared.

"Yes, but you and Diz need to get to move as a team, each one knowing what the other is asking."

For the rest of the day Lizzy and Diz walked the cloverleaf pattern over and over. Lizzy was happy to be riding again and wasn't about to complain about walking instead of running.

It was on the third day Jed finally let her do the pattern at a trot. Lizzy loved the freedom of western riding, wearing a ponytail instead of a severe bun, and jeans rather than breeches. The jeans were the best present she had ever received.

Now time seemed to fly. Every day was greeted with anticipation and excitement. Grandfather allowed no riding on weekends. It was his belief Sunday was a day of rest for both man and animals. Saturday was used for cleaning the barn, tack, animals, and home. Grandmother Elaine said she had spoiled her son terribly and wouldn't make that mistake again. Therefore, Lizzy was required to help groom the horses, clean the tack, and straighten her room. Grandmother also requested that she write her parents. At first, Lizzy balked, but since her initial letter about the ranch, each one became easier. It was as if she had learned to finally, communicate with her parents, even if it was a one-sided conversation. Jessica came in and watched Lizzy finish her letter, admiring how she had blossomed in such a short time.

"Jessie, where should I address this letter?" Lizzy asked.

"Well, let's look at the <u>itinerary</u> they left with us."

"What is today?" Lizzy inquired. "July the third." Jessie answered.

"Already! Where has the time gone?" Lizzy wondered as she applied the corresponding address of Florence, Italy, to today's date.

"I wonder if they have received any of my letters?" Lizzy remarked.

"I'm sure they have if they have stuck to their schedule. And you know your parents are always punctual!" Jessica replied.

10

New Perspectives

AT THE BREAKFAST TABLE the next morning, Grandfather had an announcement.

"Today we will be driving to the Montgomerys' for their Fourth of July celebration."

"Who are the Montgomerys?" Lizzy asked when she didn't recognize the name.

"They are the people who changed Grandmother's and my life," he answered.

"How did they do that?" Lizzy inquired.

"I met Geoffrey Montgomery in a boardroom meeting back east. You would not know he comes from one of the wealthiest families in the free world. I had never met a young man with such a sincere and respectful attitude. He wasn't cocky or full of bluster. If he didn't know something, he wasn't embarrassed to ask," Grandfather said with a hint of awe in his voice.

"Well, he sounds nice, but how did he change your life?" Lizzy asked. "We were in the middle of a very important meeting on merging our companies, when his phone vibrated. He looked at the number, excused himself and answered the call. When the call was over, he said the meeting would have to be postponed. When I asked why, he said it was a family matter. On an impulse I asked if I could accompany him. After a moment of hesitation, he said, 'Yes'. So we were out the door and on our way to his car. He looked at me and thanked me for my concern and coming with him. We drove across town to a little league field. I was flabbergasted! How dare this young whippersnapper stop an important meeting for a ball game? I could feel my blood pressure going up by the second. We parked the car and made our way hurriedly to the dugout. There on the bench with an ice pack on his face was a young lad.

"'Hey slugger, what's going on?' Geoff asked.

"The lad sat up and removed the bloody ice pack.

"'Uncle Geoff, how did you get here so fast?' the child asked.

"Geoff removed the child's ball cap to release a waterfall of red hair. Who I assumed was a boy, was a young girl. I watched his careful examination of the injured area.

"'How many fingers am I holding up?' he asked.

"She gave him the proper response; and since he was satisfied with her condition, he asked, 'Well, was he safe or out?'

"'Out! I caught the ball before he mowed me down,' she affirmed as she replaced the ice pack.

"'Well, what next?' he questioned.

"'I'm up next, but they wouldn't let me bat unless I got your okay,' she replied.

"'How do you feel?' was his gentle inquiry.

"'It only hurts when I smile, talk or laugh,' she reassured her uncle. "I'll stay while you bat. This is the last inning isn't it?' "'Yes, and we are tied.'

"'Do you want a ride home after the game?'

"'No, thank you, the team usually goes out for ice cream or something.' "'Batter up!' was called.

"When she got on the field, both teams applauded. I don't remember if she got a single or a walk, but they won by one run. Geoffrey Montgomery acted as if it were the World Series. When we got back into the car, he thanked me again for coming, and said it helped calm his nerves. His niece, Jill, was in his care during the summer while her mother and dad were on a book tour across America. Jill had a nanny and a driver but Geoff said, 'They don't take the place of family.' So he was very involved with her and her activities. He told me that call scared him to death. It was nice having a father figure with him, meaning me. I didn't tell him I couldn't even remember if my son played baseball at this age. I almost felt ashamed. He said we would reschedule the meeting, and the merger did go through. What I remember most was a comment Geoff made in the car that day. 'When it is all said and done, everything comes down to family. Nothing in the world is more important.' That simple statement hit me like a ton of bricks.

"During the following months, we saw a lot of Geoff, and he never ceased to surprise and inspire me. He asked your grandmother and me to his ranch in Kentucky for a week. That's when we met the rest of the family —— a closer, more loving family then I have ever met.

That fall, I bought Epona Estates. I felt it was time for me to get my priorities in order. Your grandmother is the most important thing in the world to me, something I took for granted for many years. It changed my life, and I have never been happier."

When they got to *Montgomery Cliffs*, Lizzy wondered how many people the Montgomerys invited. There must have been over one hundred people there for the celebration.

Lizzy couldn't hide her surprise when she found out they were all family. The amazing thing was; they seemed to like each other. From the time she got there until the end of the fireworks, she had the most fun she ever had in her life (next to riding).

11

New Teacher

LIFE SETTLED INTO A happy rhythm in the weeks that followed. Lizzy had time to weigh the difference between life of the city and country life. Each had its daily routine; however, country living was simpler and more alive. Her riding improved steadily. When Thunder had fully recovered, Grandfather found a new English riding coach through the Montgomerys. Mrs. Winsor was a tall lady with red hair and a beautiful smile. She was no nonsense when it came to teaching but never snobbish or severe. It made Lizzy love her lessons under her new teacher.

Mrs. Winsor began teaching Lizzy <u>dressage</u>. Lizzy seemed eager to learn right away. She studied the patterns at night after dinner. Grandmother would cue her on where to go step by step and at what gait. The next day was easier for Lizzy because she had studied, and now she could concentrate on executing the maneuvers. Mrs. Winsor was so impressed with Lizzy's progress she entered her and Thunder in a dressage competition. Lizzy placed third in her class.

Mrs. Winsor said it was a very respectable placing. Grandmother and Grandfather acted as if she had won the Olympics.

Lizzy was surprised when Grandfather shook Mrs. Winsor's hand to thank her for all her work with Lizzy and commented, "Jill, you have really brought Lizzy along quite nicely!"

"Grandfather, how did you know Mrs. Winsor's name was Jill? I didn't even know."

Before Grandfather could answer, Jill said, "Your Grandfather use to watch me play baseball when I was your age."

"You're *that* Jill?" Lizzy asked in amazement.

"Yes, I'm that Jill." Mrs. Winsor answered with a smile.

When not trying to master dressage maneuvers, Lizzy and Diz managed to shave a few seconds off their last run around the barrels. Now, she did them in twenty-eight seconds flat. She knew she could do better, but she respected Jed and how he spent time explaining everything. She would never do anything to jeopardize her lessons or Jed's horse Diz.

12

Possibilities

ONE SUNDAY AFTERNOON, LIZZY noticed Jed talking to her grandfather in what seemed to be a very serious conversation. Lizzy was careful not to intrude and went to the tack room to check her saddle.

That evening, Jed and Jill joined them for dinner. After a meal of barbecue ribs, dessert was served, and the conversation changed to the upcoming county fair.

"Lizzy, Honey, Jed thinks maybe you would like to show Diz in the barrel competition at the fair," Grandfather said.

"Oh, could I?" was her enthusiastic reply.

"Well, it is still five weeks away, and if you work very hard, you should be ready," he confirmed.

"I would really, really love to show Diz!"

"You must listen to *everything* Jed tells you, and do exactly as you are told."

"I will; I promise! Jed, I am so glad you thought of this!" she beamed. "I didn't; Jill did. She thought you could show both Thunder and Dizzy."

"Why are you calling him *Dizzy?*"

"It is a joke between Jed and me," Jill said with a laugh, "I like dressage, and he likes barrels. So he called my horse *Pokey*, because of the slow precision of dressage, and I called his horse *Dizzy*, because he ran around in circles."

"Well, showing both horses will be twice as great! I can't wait."

"Whoa! You have a lot of work to do before we even consider entering you. The County Fair has <u>4-H</u> and open class shows. Since you are not in 4-H, you will be showing against older, more experienced riders than you," Jed remarked.

"Older, maybe, but I have been riding and showing horses since I was six years old," she reassured her friend and instructor.

"Walk, trot, <u>canter</u> is a long way from learning a pattern to perfection, or running full out for the best time," he reminder her.

"I will work really hard; I promise!"

"Well, it's up to your grandfather and grandmother."

"Please, Grandfather!"

"Your grandmother and I have to discuss it, and we will watch you ride tomorrow, then decide," he said firmly.

13

Awaiting The Answer

IT WAS A VERY long night. Lizzy could hardly sleep because she was so excited at the prospect of showing at the fair. The odd thing about the whole thing was; she had shown many times before and had never been nervous or excited. A competition was just like another riding lesson. She was happy if she placed, but never got upset if she didn't. It was all very dignified.

Sleep finally claimed Lizzy, and her dreams took her back to her flat seat saddle, tight chignon and controlled ride. It should have been a calming dream, but morning found her tired and anxious, and she wasn't sure why.

When Lizzy got down to breakfast, Grandfather, Grandmother, and Jed were already at the table.

"I was getting ready to call you on the intercom, but I see you are eager to get an early start," Grandmother commented.

"Who are we going to ride first, Thunder or Dizzy?"

"I think we will do barrels first while the weather is still cool," was Jed's reply.

Lizzy's first attempt at the barrels was dismal at best.

"Don't give Diz his head until he is in the straightaway," Jed reminded Lizzy.

The second run was not much better than the first. "Where is your head today? It certainly isn't in riding!"

"I think I'm just tired," Lizzy sighed. "I dreamed about riding last night and the look Stefan wore on his face. He always made me feel like I was a disappointment."

"Did you always do your best?"

"I think I did. I really don't want to disappoint you, or Jill, or my grandparents."

"None of us will be disappointed if you do your very best! No half-hearted attempt will do."

"I know I've said this a lot, but I really *do* promise to do my best!" Lizzy earnestly replied.

"I know you will, so let's make the best use of our time. Get your head out of the 'what ifs' and into the here and now."

"Okay, Jed, let's give it another run."

"Hold him and wait until you are ready. Don't let him start early."

"I understand," she confirmed.

Dizzy was anxious to go, but Lizzy held him in check until she felt ready to run. Then they were off like a flash. The first barrel was a little wide, but the second was much tighter and the third one she nailed. They ran flat out toward the end where her practice paid off, with a neat turn just before they hit the gate.

Jed tried to hide his surprise at her comeback from the morning's doldrums.

He nodded his head slowly and said, "Much better." Lizzy beamed at Jed's approval.

Unknown to Jed and Lizzy, Lizzy's grandparents were watching the whole time from the golf cart.

"That was very exciting to watch, but a bit frightening. It looked dangerous," Grandmother commented with concern in her voice.

"Now, Honey, Jed is the best at this sort of riding. I'm sure he will take every precaution with Lizzy's safety," Grandfather reassured his wife.

They drove the cart to where Jed was standing. "She looks like she can handle this, what do you think, Jed?"

"If she pays attention to instructions and doesn't take any careless chances, she will do alright," Jed concurred.

"Well, Dear, we need to make a decision," reminded Grandmother. "If Jed thinks she is able; I vote yes."

"As do I, if she promises to be careful," Grandmother reiterated.

14

Stormy Night

COULD LIFE GET ANY *better?* Lizzy thought to herself. Since the weather was quite a bit warmer, Lizzy and Jill rode dressage early in the morning, then Lizzy and Jed practiced barrels late afternoon. This schedule left a large hole in the middle of the day. Every piece of tack was cleaned and polished. She studied dressage patterns until she knew them forward and backward.

Grandfather took pity on her and introduced her to his pontoon boat where they could sit in the shade and fish. The heat even affected the fishing. That night, the biggest storm Lizzy had ever experienced blew through the area. In Boston, other buildings sheltered their townhouse and bad weather of any kind rarely affected them; however, this was very different. The wind blew so hard she was positive the windows were bulging under the stress. The rain came down in torrents, and it sounded like a herd of galloping horses. Lizzy didn't want to admit it, but she was terrified. She sought out her grandparents, whom she found in the den sitting on the couch reading. She snuggled down between them, and Grandfather put his arm around her without saying anything, while Grandmother patted her on the knee. She had never felt so safe, secure, and loved in her whole life.

The morning showed the ravages of the storm. Limbs had come down, the pool was covered with debris, and some brood mares had even jumped the pasture fence.

Jed asked Lizzy if she wanted to take Diz and help with the roundup of the mares. He assured Grandfather that the mares probably hadn't gone very far. They saddled up; and on the way out to the pasture, Jed gave Lizzy her instructions.

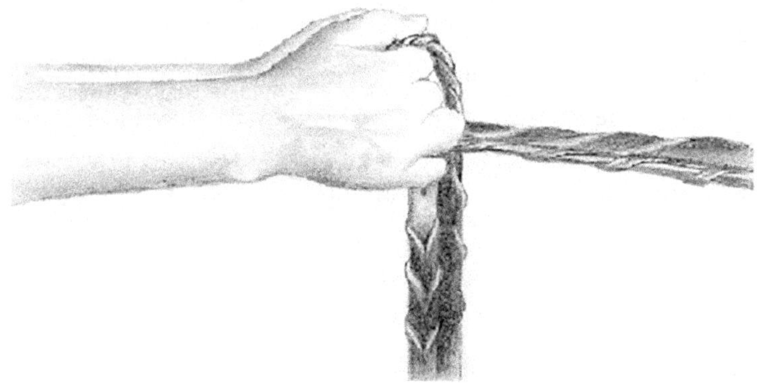

"Now, Lizzy, keep a tight grip on your reins and don't be afraid of grabbing onto the horn. Diz loves to round up horses and cows, and it will give you a chance to see how 'reining' and 'barrels' have practical uses. Watch me the first time, then you do the next one. Just remember, be calm and only use speed if the horse bolts. Got it?" He questioned.

"Got it," was Lizzy's hesitant reply.

When they came upon the first mare, she watched as Jed worked slowly and steadily until the horse <u>acquiesced</u> and returned to the pasture. They headed out to find another and came upon her by a small stream.

"You want to try?" Jed asked.

"Yes," came her simple reply.

"Okay, she's all yours."

Lizzy gave Diz a nudge, and he nearly unseated her. He was ready for action. Lizzy regained control and after several failed attempts, got the mare back to the pasture gate Jed had opened. At the end of the day, they returned to the farm with only one mare still missing.

Jed was telling Grandfather about it when a truck and trailer pulled in the front gate. Geoffrey Montgomery jumped out of the truck and went around to the back of the trailer.

"What do you have there, Geoff?" asked Grandfather.

"Well, I think I have your old <u>roan</u> mare. This crazy red head was driving my stallion nuts.

He finally jumped the fence to get at her, and I had a dickens of a time catching them. They were out frolicking like a couple of foals."

"Sorry about that. They got spooked by the storm, and we spent all day rounding them up," Jed remarked.

"I'm glad to hear you had help."

"And mighty fine help Jed was just telling me," Grandfather beamed with pride.

"That's so?" Geoff prompted.

"Lizzy got her first taste of practical horse riding. She did a good job," Jed sang Lizzy's praises.

"Great! How did you like it?" Geoff asked Lizzy.

"I loved it, no judges or timers. Diz did think it was a competition, so I had to be careful not to give him his head."

"That horse is always ready for a race!" Geoff agreed. "I came to see if you had any dinner plans. Some of our family came over when their power went out last night and stayed for the day, so we are having an <u>impromptu</u> barbecue."

"We'll be there," Grandfather promised. "Can we bring anything?"

"No, just a good appetite."

15

New Wardrobe

LIZZY LOVED EVERY MINUTE she spent with the Montgomerys. She had no idea, before this summer, families could be so large and still close. It gave her a greater appreciation for family. She loved her grandparents more than ever and basked in the affection they gave her. Lizzy wondered what it would be like if she, and her parents were close like the Montgomerys.

"Well, you ready for next week?" Geoff asked Lizzy, bringing her out of her reverie.

"What is next week?" she queried.

"The fair! Did you forget?"

"Next week, so soon? I must have lost track of time. Where has the summer gone?" she answered with amazement.

"Snuck up on you, did it?" Geoff joked.

"More than you know," Lizzy came back. With a look on her face like a deer in the headlights, she wondered, *how could the time have passed so quickly?*

On the ride home, Lizzy told her grandmother that the fair was only one week away. Grandmother Elaine got a look on her face very much like the one Lizzy wore, a cross between pain and panic.

"So soon? That will never do! We need show clothes and boots and a helmet. Oh my! How will we get everything in time?" she lamented.

"Now, Honey, we have plenty of time," Grandfather reassured his wife. When they got home, Grandmother went right to her computer to find clothes online, shouting orders to Jessica for Lizzy's measurements and sizes. A quick call was placed to Jill Winsor for a list of what was appropriate wear for dressage.

"Lizzy, Dear, let's see what you have, and we will choose what is serviceable," Grandmother instructed in a no-nonsense voice.

Lizzy seemed to have grown several inches during the summer, and after what seemed to be an endless fashion show, it was determined only her helmet was usable; everything else needed updated. At that news, Lizzy plopped down into an overstuffed chair near her grandmother, whose eyes never left the computer screen when she surprised Lizzy by saying, "Sit up, Dear, and don't slouch."

Lizzy immediately corrected her posture. The rest of the week was dedicated to acquiring all the proper clothing that would meet Elaine Pendergass' high standard of approval. The weekend was the only thing that stood between Lizzy and showing at the fair.

16

The Surprise

SHOWING WAS OLD HAT to Lizzy. She was surprised to find herself getting anxious, as the time grew short.

Like any other weekend, Saturday was set aside for cleaning stalls, tack and animals. They cleaned everything down to the last silver buckle on the bridle.

Sunday seemed to drag and fly at the same time, if that were at all possible. Meals were full of excited conversation, but the quiet time after meals dragged by slowly.

"Have you written your parents, yet?" Jessica asked.

"No. Maybe that would help pass the time," Lizzy answered.

The letter began shyly, but once Lizzy got into describing the difference between <u>tacks</u> of western riding (which she used for barrels) and dressage (which had more of an English flare) her letter seemed to write itself. Lizzy heard a commotion down stairs but didn't let it distract her from her task. When Jessica answered the knock on the door, Lizzy's attention was drawn to her grandmother's voice.

"Lizzy, Dear, there is a surprise for you downstairs," Grandmother said tentatively.

"For me? What is it?" Lizzy asked as she tore out of her room and down the stairs, only to come to an abrupt halt in front of her parents, Augustus II and Gwenith Pendergass.

"Slow down, young lady," were the first words out of her father's mouth.

"I was just writing you a letter," was her demure reply.

"Yes, we have received some very interesting letters from you. That and our conversation with Stefan when he called were monumental in our decision to return early. A great inconvenience, I might add," was Gwenith's response.

Grandfather entered the room and greeted his son and daughter-in-law. "Since it had been several years since your last visit, would you like a tour of the estate?" Gus Senior asked with pride.

"We are simply exhausted. Perhaps after we have rested," Gwenith quickly replied.

"Yes, of course, I'll show you to your rooms and have your bags brought up immediately," Elaine reassured them.

Dinner was a sedate formal affair. Conversation was amiable during the first two courses; then the mood shifted.

"It has come to my attention you, and Mother have let Elizabeth behave like a hooligan during her stay this summer. I must admit I am very disappointed," Augustus said dryly.

"I have no idea to what you are referring," Gus said defensively.

Elaine unobtrusively reached out and put her hand on her husband's arm, as if to remind him to control his temper.

"Stefan told us about her total lack of decorum and her disregard for proper attire," Gwenith stated stiffly.

"I can assure you; Elizabeth has always worn the appropriate clothes at the appropriate time," Elaine guaranteed the concerned parents.

"In her letters, she said she was riding some dizzy horse while she was wearing jeans, for heaven's sake!" Elizabeth's mother said in a huff.

"Mother, jeans are what is required when you race barrels," Elizabeth spoke for the first time during the meal. "Tomorrow at the fair, everyone who is running barrels will be in western wear."

"By no means will you be one of those people!" Gwenith was adamant. "But," Elizabeth started, then caught herself. "May I be excused?"

A curt nod from her mother released her from her dining obligation. Lizzy walked sedately from the dining room and didn't break into a run until she was out of eyesight. She ran all the way up the stairs, down the hall, right into her room, and fell onto her bed an emotional wreck. Jessica followed her up to her room.

"Oh, Jess, how could they do this to me? I have worked so hard for so long. How could they just snatch it all away from me?" Lizzy tearfully asked her caregiver and companion.

"I'm so sorry, Lizzy. It will be all right; you'll see." Jessica said trying to comfort her.

"How? The fair is tomorrow!" With those words the floodgates opened, and Lizzy sobbed into her pillow.

Downstairs, at the table the mood was tense. Both sets of Pendergasses seem to shift in their chairs and not know where to set their gaze.

Suddenly, Augustus Senior stood up and looked at his son. "I would like to see you in my study, if you would please," he added after glancing at his wife Elaine.

"Certainly." His quick acquiescence is where Lizzy got her obedience. He got out of his chair and followed his father.

Elaine, ever the consummate hostess, asked Gwenith, "Would you like to take your coffee out on the terrace?" She was trying to ease the tension in the room.

"Yes, that would be lovely," she replied.

Once on the terrace, the conversation turned to weather in Europe and other benign subjects.

In the study, the conversation was not so benign. Gus paced behind his huge mahogany desk.

He ran multi-million dollar corporations, and found it easier to talk to CEOs, than he could talk to his own son. The silence seemed to stretch on forever. Gus cleared his throat. "Son, first, and foremost, I want to say I am sorry. I feel I let you down as a father. I know I gave you everything you needed or wanted physically, but I was not very involved in your day-to-day life. I must admit, at that time in my life; my priorities were on the wrong things."

"Father, I don't know what to say," Augustus said, hesitantly.

"The thing is, Son, I don't want to see you make the same mistakes," Gus encouraged. "You have an amazing daughter. There is nothing she cannot do when she puts her mind to it. Do you know she out-fished me her first outing in a boat?"

"Frankly, Father, I was unaware that you fished at all," the younger Pendergass said with a bit of an air in his voice.

"There you go again judging, with your nose in the air. You are just like I used to be, arrogant!" Gus fumed. "Tomorrow is a very important day in your young daughter's life, and you can make it a memorable occasion or one of her life's biggest disappointments. It is up to you."

"I will talk it over with Gwenith. What time tomorrow do you need an answer?" he asked.

"If we are going to let Lizzy show tomorrow; we have to leave here by 7:30 A.M." Gus answered.

"Which show would that be? I have already given my opinion about that barrel thing," Augustus asked with his nose rising slightly in an unrelenting manner.

"Dressage, in which I might add, she has a wonderful world-class instructor," Gus said emphatically.

"I will give you an answer by 7:00 A.M. Now, if you will excuse me, it has been an exhausting day. I shall collect Gwenith and retire for the evening. I bid you good night." With that, Augustus left the study.

When Gwenith joined her husband, Elaine joined her own in the study. She entered in time to hear her husband saying to himself, "That Pompous Windbag!"

"Gus, Dear, is Lizzy going to be able to show tomorrow?" she asked. "We'll know at 7:00 A.M., and that is the best I could do, Honey," he said, shaking his head.

"I understand. Don't be so hard on yourself. It took you quite a long time to realize what was important in your life. Let's give Junior a little time," his wife said with compassion and understanding.

"Good grief, Ellie, don't let anyone hear you call our son that, or we will never hear the end of it!" Gus said, ushering his wife out of the study as he chuckled under his breath.

"I won't be able to sleep a wink until I know what tomorrow will bring." Elaine's concern could be heard in her voice.

17

Change of Plans

LIZZY TOOK THE FACT that the sunshine had to fight its way through the clouds as an omen. Her spirit was as <u>tumultuous</u> as the sky outside her window. Jessica had laid out a pair of slacks and a nice shirt for her to wear, another reminder that her carefree summer, of jean-clad, riding was over. It was all she could do to put the clothes on. Even her walk reflected her dampened spirit.

She arrived at the breakfast table at 7:00 A.M.

Her parents and grandparents were already seated. Her father glanced at his watch to ensure she was on time. A curt nod of approval was her morning greeting.

"Good morning, Dear," were the first words she heard. These words helped her relax. At least, her grandmother hadn't changed. "What would you like for breakfast?" Grandmother inquired.

"May I have a bagel, please?" Lizzy answered.

"Yes, of course. Would you like both milk and juice?" Grandmother prodded, knowing today's busy schedule would take much nourishment.

"Yes, thank you," Lizzy answered quietly, her eyes downcast.

Elaine had a flashback to a small boy sitting at her table looking the same way. *Life is full of "if-only-I-knew-then-what-I-know-now"*, she thought to herself. She patted her husband on the shoulder, seeming to cement their resolve not to let this happen to Lizzy.

"Elizabeth, I am sure you are wondering whether or not you will be showing today. Your mother and I have discussed it and have decided you may show in dressage," her father affirmed.

"Thank you, Sir," Lizzy responded. It seemed she began eating with a little more gusto and was sitting a bit taller.

Elaine took it as a sign of her beginning to feel like herself again and commented, "We must hurry if you want to warm Thunder up before you show."

"What time does she show?" Gwenith inquired.

"The dressage starts at nine, and the barrels begin at five." Gus answered. "You misunderstood; she will be showing only in dressage," his son reiterated.

"I understand," Gus responded. He looked up only to find Elaine had left the room. He hoped she was not upset.

"We will meet you in time for the show," Gwenith informed them.

"May I be excused?" Lizzy asked, trying to curb her enthusiasm, which seemed to be bubbling under the surface. She was excited to be going to the fair, even if it was only for dressage. This was going to be her first fair ever!

When they were ready to leave, Lizzy asked her grandfather, "May I ride with Jed in the truck?"

"Yesterday I would have said, 'Yes,' but you and I both know things have changed. To be on the safe side, let's do things according to Hoyle." He explained.

"Who is Hoyle?" Lizzy asked.

Grandfather chuckled, "Hoyle is a person who wrote a book of rules for card games in the 1700's. This book was considered the law of card playing. The phrase, 'according to Hoyle' was started then, and became a catch phrase for doing things right ever since."

"Oh," she said, accepting his explanation.

To Lizzy's surprise, Jake drove up in her grandfather's regular Lincoln Navigator SUV. Jessica was in the front seat with him. Lizzy looked at her grandfather to see his reaction, but he just opened the door for his wife, and Lizzy got in behind them.

"According to Hoyle?" Lizzy asked.

"Yes, but without airs. It is, after all, a county fair." He winked at Lizzy.

Jed left with the truck and the horse trailer, and everyone else followed.

To help pass the time it took to get to the fairgrounds, Grandmother quizzed Lizzy on her dressage pattern. As they neared the entrance, Grandfather cleared his throat, then said, "Lizzy, I'm sorry about not riding in the barrel competition."

"It's okay. I got to ride Dizzy around the barrels all summer. I just can't show. I do feel as though I am letting Jed down."

"I'm sure he understands," her grandfather reassured her.

They drove through the gate without stopping. Gus had Jed get passes for the whole week of the fair so the gate attendant just waved them through.

Lizzy checked in, then went to the <u>arena</u>, and <u>warmed up</u> Thunder. Their horse trailer was equipped with living quarters, so that is where Lizzy went to get ready for the show after the warm-up was over.

"How do you feel?" Grandmother Pendergass asked, as she watched Jessica put Lizzy's hair in a tight chignon, finishing it off with her helmet.

"As many times as I have shown, you would think I wouldn't get nervous, but I am a little anxious. I can't remember the last time Mother, and Father watched me ride or show. I don't want to do anything to embarrass them," was Lizzy's thoughtful reply.

"Honey, there is nothing in this world you could do to embarrass any of us!" her grandmother said emphatically.

"We know you will do your best like you always do, Lizzy." Jessica added for encouragement.

"That is all anyone could ever ask," Grandmother reaffirmed. "Do you have her number, Jessica?"

"Yes, right here," Jessica said as she pinned the number on the back of Lizzy's suit jacket.

As many years as Lizzy had been showing, this time she felt different. She actually felt the love from her grandparents and Jake and Jessica. She knew her parents loved her, but this filled her and gave her a new resolve to make them all proud. A knock on the door made her come back to reality.

"Is she ready to go?" her instructor Jill queried. "I watched her warm up, and she looked good,"

"I'm ready," Lizzy said as she emerged from the trailer.

"Well, let's go over the pattern one more time," Jill encouraged.

"Okay, ask away." Lizzy's excitement was <u>palatable</u>.

After the review,they made their way to the arena where the show was to be held. They found Thunder's stall, where Jed was talking to Jake.

"I got you a program in case you wanted an extra," Jed told Jill. "Thanks, I do like to keep score on one."

"What about this afternoon? Any word about riding?" Jed asked.

"No, their foolish pride probably won't let them change their minds!"

Grandmother interjected with more venom than she intended.

"Well, the day is not over, yet. There is still room for hope. A little prayer wouldn't hurt either," Jed said, always optimistic. "Let's see what number they are at in the lineup."

Gwenith and Augustus arrived with their usual flair, dressed in designer slacks and cardigans tied just right around their necks. They found their way to their seats in the Coliseum, near the elder Pendergasses, and wiped the imaginary dust off the seats before they sat. There was boredom written on their faces, the young Pendergasses being poster children for the emotion. As the next rider showed, they seemed to come out of a fog and act semi-interested. After each consecutive rider, they sat a little straighter and watched a little more intently. Lizzy was the next rider up, and Gwenith very uncharacteristically grabbed her husband's arm. He, in like manner, put his hand over hers. After a nod to the judges, Lizzy started her pattern. Gwenith's other hand fluttered to her throat when Lizzy did her sidesteps in precise form. By the end of her performance, Gwenith was beside herself with worry and excitement. She looked over at Elaine and Gus and asked, "How do you think she did? I thought she was brilliant!" Gwenith didn't even try to hide the pride in her voice.

"It is very hard to tell since all the riders seem to be doing remarkably well," Gus answered on the side of caution.

"Why were some so much older than she was?" Augustus asked.

"This is an open show, and any age may enter." Elaine explained.

"When will we know how she did?" asked Lizzy's mother.

"After the last rider shows, they will announce the placing," Gus Senior answered.

"How many are left?" Lizzy's father asked.

"According to the program, five," said Elaine.

Sitting through the last of the riders seemed to take an eternity. Then the wait while the judges tallied the scores was torturous.

The announcer came on with comments on the fine show. He was handed the tally sheet and began, "Ladies and Gentlemen; our judges have finished the scoring, and the places are as follows: fifth place goes to number 78, Sally Creek. Fourth place goes to number 8, Howard Jones. Third place goes to number 1, Franklin Kroger. Second place goes to number 14, Elizabeth Pendergass. And our First-place winner goes to number 22, Grace Overton! We congratulate everyone on an excellent show."

Gwenith never heard anything after her daughter's name. She was on her feet yelling "Bravo, bravo!", much to her husband's surprise. Many odd looks came from the fairgoers in the stands. By the time they gathered together after the ribbons were awarded, Gwenith and Augustus were smiling ear-to-ear.

"Very well done!" Lizzy's mother patted her shoulder. Lizzy was so happy that her mother's odd behavior was lost on her. Jill met them and gave Lizzy a big hug, telling her she was very proud in the process.

"Thank you," Lizzy said through a huge grin.

"She did splendidly, didn't she?" Gwenith beamed at Jill.

"Yes, she did," Jill concurred.

"Now, what time is her next show?" Gwenith asked getting caught up in the excitement. After everyone stopped talking and looked at her, she became conscious of what she had blurted out. Blinking a couple of times, she fixed her eyes on her husband and said, "May I have a word with you?"

"Of course," he replied, as they moved out of earshot.

"What was that all about?" Augustus demanded.

"This is what I remember from my childhood, before we moved to Boston, and snobbery replaced fun. We use to go to the county fairs and festivals. What we do now is laugh at what is supposed to be funny, or should I say humorous? When was the last time you enjoyed yourself? I mean, really enjoyed yourself? How did you feel watching Elizabeth show? Were you excited and proud? When was the last time anything or anyone made you feel that way? Have you noticed how much she has grown? We missed it. Her growing into a young adult didn't happen overnight. Well, I don't want to miss anymore." Once Gwenith got going, she could hardly stop all the feelings she had buried for so many years.

Everyone stood back, trying not to stare at the heated exchange going on between Lizzy's parents. The tension in the air was thick.

"I don't know where this is coming from? What are you talking about?" Augustus said bewilderedly.

"Let me ask you this. What was your favorite part about Europe this year?" Gwenith asked.

"I enjoyed all of it," he said a little defensively.

"You can't name one thing. The most exciting thing for me was learning from Stefan, we had a reason to come home!" she said, raising her voice enough to carry to the nervous group awaiting the outcome of this discussion.

Augustus stood dumbfounded. "I had no idea you felt this way. Why didn't you say something sooner?"

"Because I didn't ever want to do anything to disappoint you" she said in a soft, sad voice. She dabbed the moisture that threatened to spill from her eyes.

It was so unlike Gwenith to be upset; Augustus didn't know how to respond, so he wrapped his arms around her. Elizabeth's mouth dropped open at the public display of affection in which her parents were engaged.

"So, what do you want to do?" he asked gently.

"Let's just enjoy the day and see what our daughter is capable of," she petitioned her husband.

"Are you sure?" he asked as he released her.

She nodded, and they walked back to the group hand in hand.

"Elizabeth, we have decided to let you show the dizzy horse," her father explained.

"Really? Oh, thank you! Thank you! Thank you!" was Lizzy's enthusiastic response.

"Well, we have a little time, so let's go to the Chuck Wagon Café and get some lunch," Gus senior suggested.

"I'm too nervous to eat," Lizzy insisted.

"You can get something to drink," Grandmother coaxed.

Once they got to the café, Lizzy ended up eating a foot-long hot dog, a fried flower onion, and a pop.

"Why don't you and Jessica go back to the trailer and rest a while. We'll come get you when it is time to warm up Diz," her grandmother urged.

18

The Final Show

AS PROMISED, GRANDMOTHER PENDERGASS came into the trailer and woke up Lizzy.

"I can't believe I fell asleep! I was so worked up; I didn't think I could even begin to rest," Lizzy said in amazement.

"Let's get you changed into your western wear and number." Jessica rose from her chair at Elaine's suggestion.

Lizzy was unsure of what she was feeling, anxious, happy, or confused. Her parents were not acting normal. They almost seemed relaxed, which was very much out of character. But they said she could show, and she was not about to question the whys and wherefores. Getting her head out of the clouds and back to the show was what she needed to do now, and the rest would take care of itself. Ready for the show, Lizzy left the trailer. Jed had Diz saddled by the time they got to his stall. Warming up Diz helped Lizzy focus. She and Diz seemed to be riding as one unit. He was sensitive to her every cue. Around the barrels in the practice arena they went, each time faster than the time before.

"I think that is enough for now," Jed told Lizzy. "You and Diz should rest a few minutes before it's your turn."

"Okay." Lizzy didn't even consider questioning the suggestion. One of Lizzy's best attributes was her obedience.

Waiting was always the hardest part of showing. Once she was showing, she was focused; but waiting allowed time for her mind to wander. To keep that from happening, Lizzy watched the other riders intently. She noticed every time a horse went around the second barrel, it seemed to slide and struggle in the deep sand. Lizzy stored that information away. Before long her number was called, and she was at the gate. She could feel the tension in Diz, but knew not to give him his head too early. She couldn't afford to run past the first barrel, or to knock over any barrels. All the riders before her were doing very well.

Now it was their turn. Away they flew, starting the timer. Diz was in his element from years of showing with Jed, circling the first barrel nice and tight. He waited for the cue from Lizzy at the second barrel. Diz was anxious to take the turn tight, but Lizzy kept their circle a little wide. The third barrel was as tight as the first, and she gave Diz his head in the straightaway. Lizzy was relieved to finish without penalties, and hoped the wide turn didn't cost her too much time. Her main concern had been to keep Diz safe. She knew what he meant to Jed, and wouldn't chance a fall in deep sand. Jed was at the gate to help Lizzy off the excited horse.

"You did a great job, Lizzy; I noticed your second turn was a little wide," was Jed's observation.

"I noticed the other horses were slipping there, and were scrambling to regain their footing. I didn't want Diz to get hurt," she reasoned.

Jed was touched by her concern for his old friend. He also knew the turn would probably cost her a second or two.

An excited voice distracted her from her conversation with Jed. Her parents and grandparents were making their way toward her.

"Elizabeth! That was amazing!" Her mother exclaimed, too excited to wait until she was in front of her daughter to convey her sentiments.

The grin on her father's face seemed out of place, but Lizzy liked the way it looked.

"I've never been so scared in all my life. You literally flew around those barrel things. I have never seen anyone ride a horse that fast except jockeys in a horse race." The words spilled from Gwenith's mouth.

"Are you alright? Your mother is right in her assessment of the speed. I found it to be quite exhilarating," her father added.

"I am quite fine, thank you. Did you enjoy the show?" Lizzy asked hesitantly.

"We enjoyed it very much, and to think we nearly missed it by being prejudice about western riding," Lizzy's mother confessed.

Elaine came over to tell them that the placing was being announced. Then, they all gathered by the gate to hear the results. When Lizzy Pendergass and Dexter's Impressive Zip were called, Jed gave Lizzy a knee up into the saddle so she could go in and receive her Third Place ribbon. Her parents and grandparents were so proud you would have thought she had won first place. Lizzy was so happy she thought her heart would burst.

They all walked around the fairgrounds together, talking amiably. Lizzy even went on a fair ride or two, something she had never done before. Lizzy didn't think life could get any better.

19

New Beginnings

WHEN THEY GOT HOME that night, everyone was tired, so they all went their bedrooms. Jessica was helping Lizzy when a knock got their attention. Jessica answered, surprised to see Lizzy's parents. Jessica invited them to sit down and excused herself to give them privacy.

"If you are not too tired, we would like to talk to you," Gwenith said.

"Of course, Mother," Lizzy answered.

"As you know, we were to be in Europe until the school year started. And it was our intent when we came here to take you back there with us. Your father and I had a nice long talk today and again in the car on the return trip to the ranch. We have come to an agreement, if it's all right with you, we will stay here for the rest of the summer." Unsure of how this news would be received; Gwenith clenched her hands on her lap.

"Oh, Mother! That would make me so happy! I could show you and father how to fish, and introduce you to the Montgomerys," and the floodgates opened to the excited ramblings of Elizabeth Epona Pendergass.

The rest of the summer flew by, and Lizzy and her parents grew to know each other better day-by-day. Her parents saw the wisdom of the elder Pendergass, in the belief that family is the most important thing in the world. This summer at Epona Estates was a very special time and place for everyone, especially Lizzy 'N Dizzy.

By Joyce M. Lambert

Definitions

4-H	a youth organization whose mission is "engaging youth to reach their fullest potential while advancing the field of youth development". Its name is a reference to the occurrence of the initial letter H four times in the organization's original motto 'head, heart, hands, and health'.
accolades	strong praise or approval; acclaim.
acquiesce	to accept something reluctantly but without protest.
arena	an enclosed area for the presentation of sports events and spectacles.
bell boots	are a type of protective boot worn by a horse. They encircle the horse's ankle, and protect the back of the pastern and the heels of the animal.
canter	a smooth gait, especially of a horse, that is slower than a gallop but faster than a trot.
cajole	to persuade someone to do something by sustained coaxing or flattery.
decorum	propriety, esp. in behavior, or conduct.

| demerit | a mark made against one's record for a fault or for misconduct. |

| dressage | the guiding of a horse through a series of complex maneuvers by slight movements of the rider's hands, legs, and weight |

Epona (possibly Roman mythology) — Celtic goddess of horses and mules and asses.

equestrian — of or relating to horseback riding or horseback riders.

farrier — a craftsman who trims and shoes horses' hooves.

forging — of a horse at a trot, the front feet being struck by the back feet, making a forging sound.

have his head — letting him take the bit and run.

impromptu — prompted by the occasion rather than being planned in advance.

indecorously — lacking propriety or good taste.

itinerary — a planned route or journey.

Liz Taylor — Elizabeth Taylor - She began as a child actress in the early 1940s, and was one of the most popular stars of classical Hollywood. She starred in National Velvet in 1944.

muck bucket — large bushel type bucket used for hauling refuse from horse stalls.

palatable — acceptable or agreeable to the mind or sensibilities.

roan — of the color sorrel, chestnut, or bay, sprinkled with gray or white.

splint boots	support and help protect horse's legs from injury.
tack	equipment, such as saddles and harnesses, for horses.
thoroughbred	originating from a cross between Arabian stallions and English mares.
tumultuous	uproarious, riotous, or turbulent.
warming up	to prepare for an athletic event by exercising, stretching, or practicing for a short time beforehand.

Keep reading for a preview of

'Bonnie 'N Clyde.'

Bonnie 'N Clyde

ER MOM THOUGHT IT would be a good idea for her to get out of her rut. Yea! Right! What rut? Just because she liked hanging out with her friends and go to the mall or movies didn't sound like a rut to her. Okay, she admits; she may spend a little too much time on her cell phone, but that doesn't constitute a rut either!

"Just shoot me now!" Bonnie said with all the drama she felt, as she launched herself backwards onto her bed.

"It will be good for you to see a different way of life, and learn to appreciate what you have," her mom cajoled.

"You can't be serious about this! I am not a little girl anymore! I don't need to be sent away to a summer camp!" Bonnie protested.

"Oh, I promise, this is nothing like a summer camp. We are letting you visit some old friends of ours. They have kids your age." She reassured her 15-year-old daughter.

"How come I don't know these people if they are such good friends of yours?" Bonnie asked.

"Well, we just got busy with life, but you do know them. You will be going to stay with the Smuckers." Her mom said quietly.

"You have got to be crazy! I am not going to spend my whole summer in Amishville!!" She cried.

She cried and cried, and ranted, raved and pouted. However, nothing would change her parent's minds.

The school term ended and summer vacation began, for her friends, but not her. Bonnie thought her mother had relented when she suggested they go to the mall. Bonnie needed a good shot of the mall to take her mind off her troubles.

The day she dreaded arrived. She was packed with all her new mall clothes her mom bought for her trip. Her plain clothes. Shirts, with no bedazzlement, or pictures or words. New jeans, with plain everything, for every day. She even got new dresses, not fancy or bright or bedazzled either, just plain dresses in dull drab colors for Sundays. It was all just too much. The worst-case scenario was true. No change of mind. No mall with friends, no movies, no cell phone. Torture, pure and simple.

This summer promised to be the worst summer of her life. The two-hour drive went way too fast. They were there in no time at all.

"Mom, please, let's just stay for a nice day visit, and all go home." Bonnie pleaded.

"This will be a summer you will remember the rest of your life." mom reassured.

"Oh, I believe that! It will be the thing horror movies are made about!" After a nice day her parents prepared to leave, and Bonnie panicked. "Mom, please, I promise I will be good, please do not do this to me!" She resisted getting down on her knees.

"Don't make a scene Bonnie. I gave your phone to Mary, and she will let you call home on Sundays. Be good and have fun. We love you!" Her dad and mom gave her hugs and kisses then they were gone.

Bonnie didn't know where to go or what to do. She knew she didn't want to be here. Kids her age, that was a joke, there were some older and younger, ten in all. It was very different from her solitary life of an only child. How was she going to survive the summer? Maybe she could run away to one of her friends? But it was getting dark, so it would have to wait until morning. Mary and the girls showed Bonnie to her room and were to put her things. Bonnie got ready for bed and laid there a long time listening to the sounds of the night. The snoring, coughing, soft mumbles, crickets, owls and whatever was stomping outside. She finally turned over and tried not to cry. But, truth be told, her pillow was damp from her tears.

Chapter 2

WHAT IS THAT NOISE? Someone was coming up the stairs in the middle of the night. What should she do? Hide under the bed? In the closet? "Bonnie, it's time to get up." said the voice on the other side of the door.

The plea was repeated, "Bonnie, it is time to get up."

"It's the middle of the night!" Bonnie observed.

"No, it is 5:00am, time to milk the cows," the voice clarified.

"Do what?" Bonnie bolted upright in bed. "You have got to be kidding."

Mary opened the door. "I assure you I am not kidding, come along." Though she spoke quietly you could tell she brooked no nonsense.

Like ducks to the pond, one by one, the children filed out of the house toward the barn. There the older ones each took a one-legged stool and a bucket, sat and began to milk. The smaller ones got a scoop of feed for each cow. Bonnie was unsure what she should do, so she grabbed a stool and a bucket, but she really had no idea how to milk a cow. Sara, the oldest girl, saved the day by coming over with a full pail of milk.

"If you will take the full pail and pour it into the milk can in the milk house; you won't have to milk."

"Thank you!" Bonnie gushed, because she was really thankful, she didn't have to get down in the 'yuck' to milk. Just as she was pouring her second bucket, it started. The most beautiful music she had ever heard. She walked back into the barn to hear where the sound was coming from, after all they were not supposed to have radios. All the children were singing a song with a sweet melody and harmonizing with perfection. She was so enthralled, she couldn't move, for fear of breaking the magic of the moment. Someone handed her a full bucket, and she relinquished her empty. Everything fell into an almost hypnotic rhythm, and time flew by. She couldn't even tell how many buckets she had emptied. Time just went by as each person did the job they were given, not complaining, or slacking off, just singing and getting things done. Before Bonnie realized the buckets stopped coming and things were put away. Then, the little duck procession went back to the house for breakfast.

About the Author

JOYCE LAMBERT HAS BEEN published author for over thirty years. She began as a poet, but has since branched out into children's literature, publishing her first book, *SLICK 'N SLIDE*. Joyce lives on a farm with Jim, her husband of nearly fifty years, where they raised six children, assorted horses and many other animals. There the farm life, the beauty of the Indiana countryside, and the bordering Kankakee River, have been a constant inspiration for the stories she writes for her twenty one grandchildren.

About the Illustrator

JANET METZGER HARTWIG HAS been drawing most of her life, pencil being her favorite medium. This is her second book with Joyce Lambert. Janet has ridden horses since childhood, and loves barrel racing, competing in local shows and rodeos. She is an OR nurse, and enjoys running in her spare time. She lives on *FAST LANE FARMS* in Valparaiso, Indiana with her husband Mark and their three children.

* 9 7 8 1 7 3 3 4 3 9 6 4 0 *